High Win Rate Momentum Trading Strategies

Strategies for Capturing Big Wins in the Crypto, Forex and Stock Market Using Momentum

Copyright ©

All rights reserved. No part of this book may be reproduced, stored in a retrieval system, or transmitted in any form or by any means, electronic, mechanical, photocopying, recording, scanning, or otherwise, without the prior written permission of the publisher.

Disclaimer

This book is not to be used for financial advice.

All the material contained in this book is provided for informational purposes only. The author does not guarantee any results from the use of this information.

No responsibility can be taken for any results or outcomes resulting from the use of this material.

While every attempt has been made to provide information that is both accurate and effective, the author does not assume any responsibility for the accuracy or use/misuse of this information.

Table of Contents

Introduction   1

Chapter 1: Identifying and Using Momentum in Trading   2

Chapter 2: Momentum and Market Trends   9

Chapter 3: Identifying Winning Momentum Setups   19

Chapter 4: The Best TradingView Momentum Indicator Signals   30

Chapter 5: Momentum Trading Strategies   54

Conclusion   76

Introduction

Welcome to the ultimate guide to mastering momentum trading! This book is your one-stop-shop for everything you need to know about using momentum indicators and strategies to make profitable trades in the market.

In the first chapter, we dive deep into the world of momentum indicators, showing you exactly how to use them to identify potential buying or selling opportunities and the different types of signals they can provide. We'll also teach you the importance of using multiple indicators in conjunction with each other to gain a more comprehensive understanding of market conditions.

Moving on to chapter 2, we'll explore the relationship between momentum and market trends, covering the different types of trends that traders may encounter and providing techniques for identifying strong momentum and trends. We'll also reveal the secrets of market reversals and how momentum plays a key role in these critical turning points.

In chapter 3, we'll take you step-by-step through the process of analyzing the market and identifying opportunities. From assessing risk and reward, to identifying good entries and exits using momentum indicators, we'll arm you with the knowledge and tools you need to make smart, profitable trades.

Chapter 4 is where the real magic happens. We've scoured the markets and handpicked the best TradingView momentum indicator signals for you. We'll show you how to use these indicators to generate buy and sell signals, and provide examples of how to use these indicators in real-world trading scenarios.

Finally, in chapter 5, we'll reveal our most powerful and highly profitable momentum trading strategies. From TSI + DEMA to Double MACD, UT Bot + KDJ, TMO + Hull, Williams %R Scalping and more, these strategies have been tried, tested and proven to deliver results.

Get ready to take your trading to the next level with this comprehensive guide to momentum trading.

By following the techniques and strategies outlined in this book, you'll be able to develop a more effective approach that is tailored to your individual needs and goals. Now let's get started!

Chapter 1: Identifying and Using Momentum in Trading

How Momentum can be used as an "Edge" in Trading

Momentum can provide valuable insight into the potential future movement of a security or market.

One of the most important things to know about using momentum in trading is that changes in momentum will typically precede changes in price. This can make momentum a "leading indicator", meaning it can be used to predict price movements.

Let's say you're trading bitcoin and you notice that there has been on an upward trend for the past few weeks. You decide to buy in, hoping to ride the trend for a bit longer.

But how do you know if the trend is likely to continue or if it's about to reverse?

This is where momentum comes in, we can use momentum to predict whether the trend will continue or reverse based on how strong the momentum is, and whether it's increasing or decreasing.

Increasing/Strong Momentum

- If the market has strong momentum in a particular direction, it is more likely to continue moving in that direction, at least in the short term.

Decreasing/ Weakening Momentum

- When the momentum starts to weaken or stall, it may be an indication that the trend is starting to lose steam and a reversal could be on the horizon.

Using Momentum Indicators

Momentum indicators can be incredibly useful for traders, as they allow for the identification of both robust trends as well as early indications of a trend reversal by measuring the rate at which momentum is increasing or decreasing.

Momentum indicators calculate the rate of change in price over a certain period of time. This calculation is typically done by comparing the current price to a previous price, such as the closing price from a specific number of periods ago.

The resulting calculation, which is typically represented as a ratio or percentage, is then plotted on a chart. This creates a visual representation of the momentum of the financial instrument, which traders can use to identify trends and potential trend reversals.

There are several different types of momentum indicators, each of which uses a slightly different calculation to measure momentum.

Some popular examples include:

- Relative strength index (RSI)
- Moving Average Convergence Divergence (MACD)
- Stochastic Oscillator (SO)

Each of these indicators has its own unique way of plotting the momentum value.

Momentum indicators are typically composed of several key components that traders use to assess the strength and direction of a trend.

Types of Momentum Indicator Signals

Below we will take a look at the types of signals that can be found on momentum indicators

Centerline Cross

The centerline is a horizontal line that is used as a reference point on the indicator's chart. For many momentum indicators, this line is set at a value of 50, but it can be different depending on the indicator.

Values above the centerline indicate that momentum is increasing and prices are rising, while values below the centerline indicate that momentum is decreasing and prices are falling.

- If the momentum indicator crosses or is above 50, this indicates a uptrend is occurring or imminent

- If momentum indicator crosses or is below the centerline, this indicates a downtrend is occurring or imminent

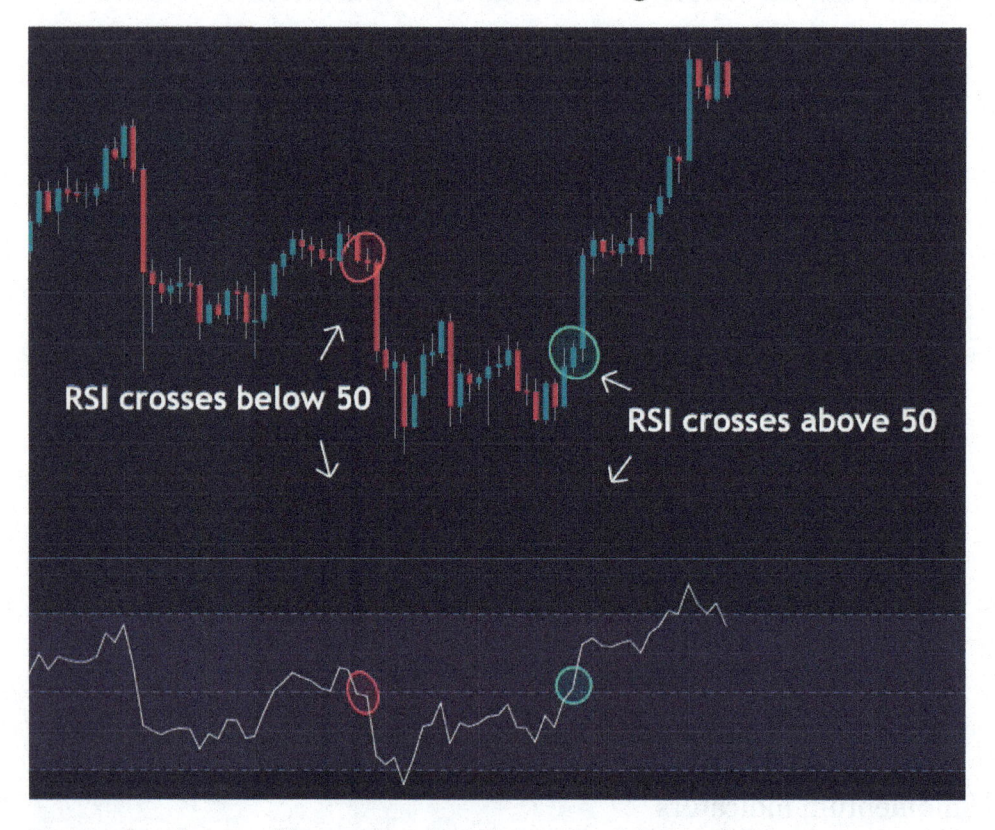

Example of centerline cross signals on the RSI

Overbought/Oversold

Another important component of momentum indicators are the overbought and oversold zones.

These are designated areas above or below the centerline that indicate that the financial instrument's price may be reaching an extreme level, and a reversal is likely.

- **Oversold**: Usually below 30, this indicates price has fallen too quickly and is likely to bounce

- **Overbought:** Typically above 70, this indicates price has risen too rapidly and a pull back is likely.

When using overbought/oversold signals it is important to know that these signals are unreliable in strong trending markets, and the momentum indicator can remain in these zones for an extended period of time.

For this reason it is best to use these signals in sideways/ranging markets, it is also important to wait for the indicator to exit the OB/OS zone before using it as a valid signal.

Divergence

Divergence is another important concept when using momentum indicators. Divergence occurs when the price of a financial instrument and the indicator's value are moving in opposite directions.

There are two types of divergence to be aware of for predicting trend reversals, these are – bullish divergence and bearish divergence.

Bullish divergence:

Price makes a lower low, yet the indicator makes a higher low. This may indicate that the downward trend is losing strength and a potential reversal is coming.

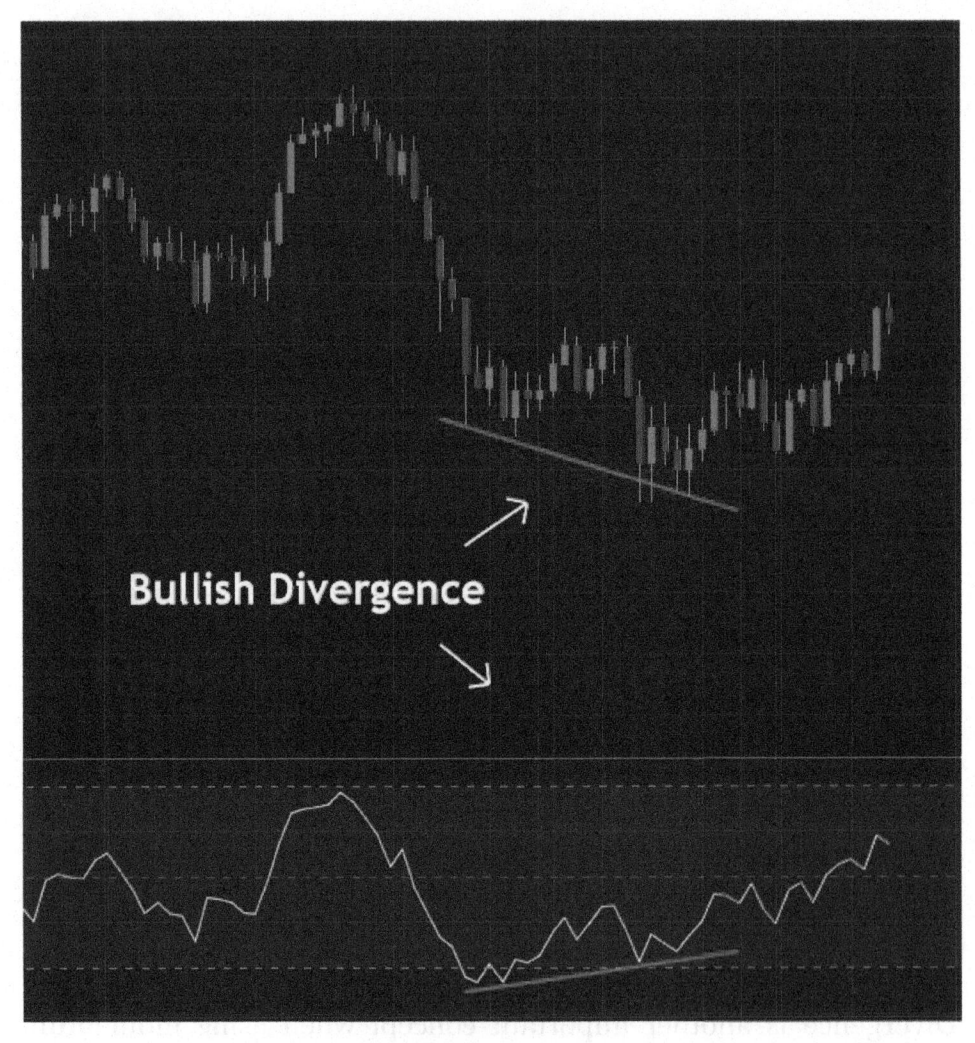

Example of bullish divergence on the RSI

Bearish Divergence:

Price makes a higher high, but the indicator makes a lower high, this may indicate that the upward trend is losing strength and a potential reversal is coming.

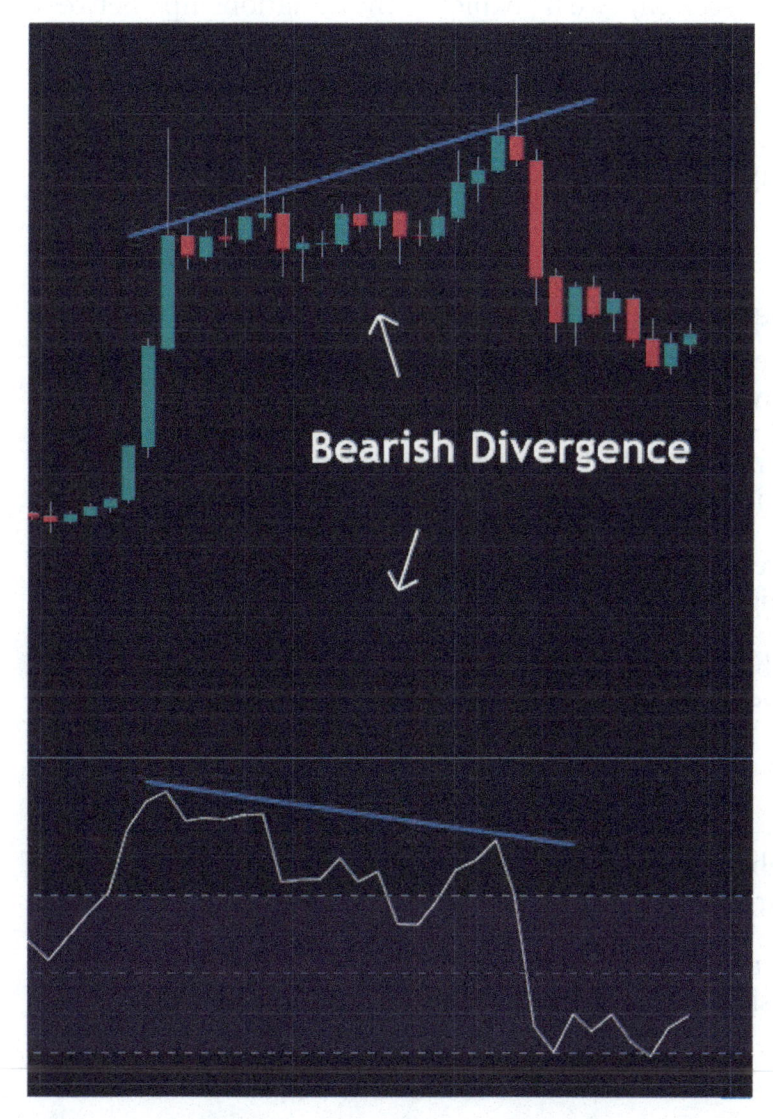

Example of bearish divergence on the RSI

Chapter 2: Momentum and Market Trends

In the world of trading, momentum and market trends go hand in hand. In this section, we'll explore the relationship between momentum and market trends and discuss how traders can use momentum to identify trends and make informed decisions.

First, let's define market trends. A trend is a general direction in which a security or market is moving.

Types of Trends

Trends can be bullish (upward), bearish (downward), or range-bound (sideways).

- Bull trends/up trends are characterized by a series of higher highs and higher lows
- Bear trends/down trends are characterized by a series of lower highs and lower lows.
- Range-bound trends are characterized by a series of highs and lows that are relatively close together

So how does momentum fit into the picture?

Momentum is a measure of the strength of a price move and can provide valuable insight into the potential future direction of a security or market.

By analyzing momentum, traders can identify trends and make informed decisions about when to enter or exit a trade.

How to Identify Strong Trending Markets

When it comes to trading, one of the most profitable opportunities is trading strong trending markets. In these types of market conditions, price will be rapidly trending either up or down. If you are on the right side of this trend you can make massive gains very quickly.

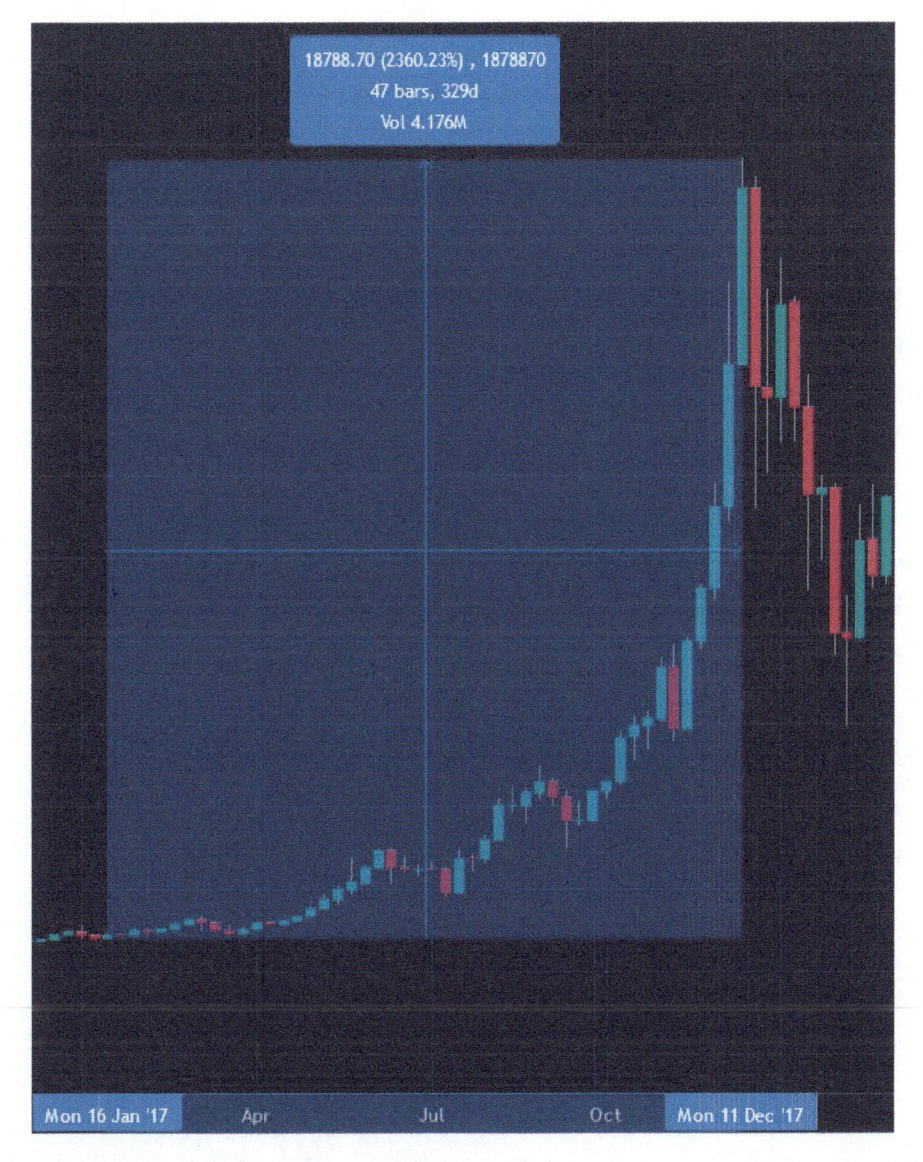

The infamous 2017 bitcoin bull market

A good example of this was the crazy 2017 bitcoin bull market, from Jan 2017 to Dec 2017 bitcoin rose by more than 2300%!

Typically when the market is in a strong trend, you can ride the trend without having to worry about it reversing on you. As you can see from the example above, these types of market trends can be hugely profitable if you enter at the right time.

But how can you find these types of insane price moves before it's too late? Momentum can help us find these types of strong trends early and allow us to get in them early before they take off when using the right techniques.

Techniques for Identifying Strong Momentum and Trends

Below are some highly effective methods for identifying strong momentum and market trends.

Moving Average Slopes

Moving averages are a type of technical indicator that smooth out price data by calculating the average price of an asset over a certain period of time (e.g., 20 days, 50 days, 200 days).

When the moving average is sloping upwards, it indicates an uptrend, and when it is sloping downwards, it indicates a downtrend. The steeper the moving average is slopped the higher the momentum is.

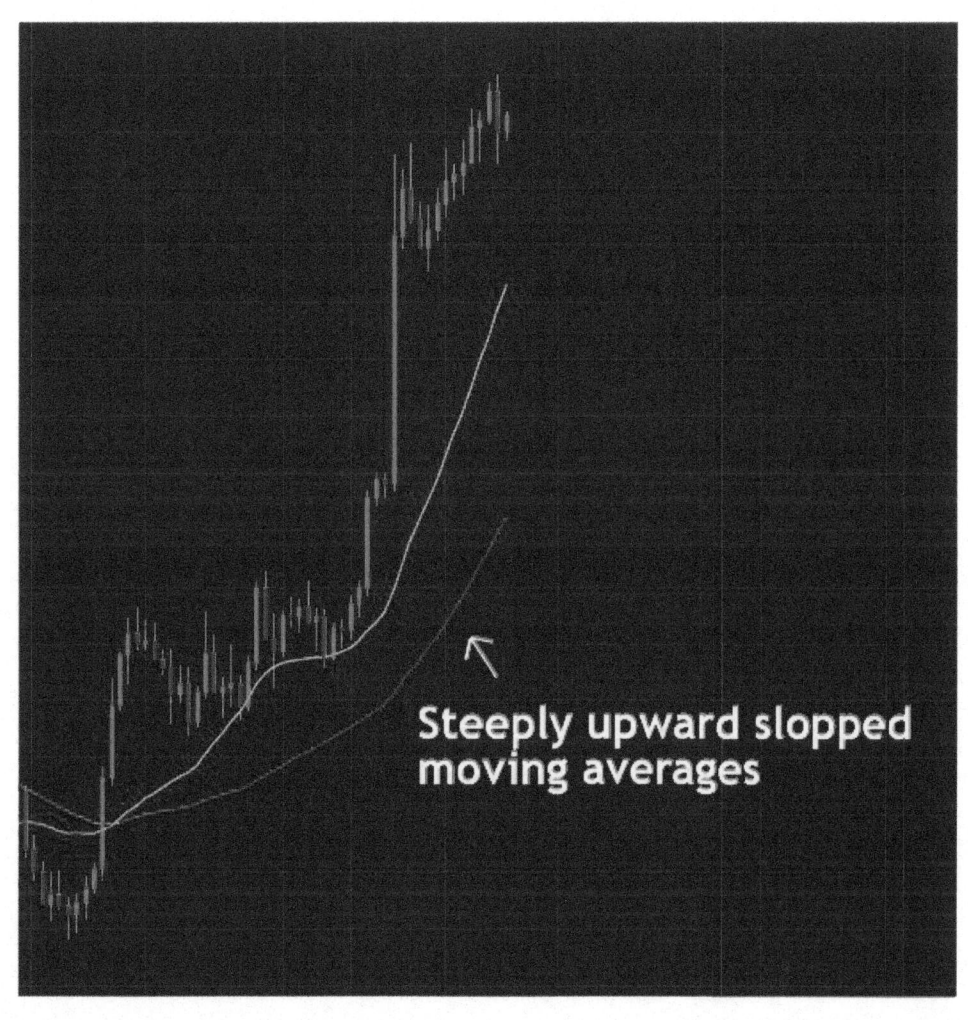

Example of steeply upward slopped moving averages indicating strong upward momentum

Another thing that will occur with moving averages is the faster moving averages will spread further away from the longer period moving averages. For example, if a 20 period EMA is far away from the 50 EMA, this indicates strong momentum.

Trend lines

Trend lines are diagonal lines that are drawn on a chart to connect a series of highs or lows. There are two types of trend lines - uptrend lines and downtrend lines.

1. **Uptrend lines:** An uptrend line is drawn by connecting a series of lows on a chart. When the price of an asset is consistently making higher highs and higher lows, it is said to be in an uptrend.

   An uptrend line is drawn by connecting the lows on the chart and extending it out into the future. As long as the price remains above the uptrend line, the uptrend is considered to be intact.

2. **Downtrend lines:** A downtrend line is drawn by connecting a series of highs on a chart. When the price of an asset is consistently making lower highs and lower lows, it is said to be in a downtrend.

   A downtrend line is drawn by connecting the highs on the chart and extending it out into the future. As long as the price remains below the downtrend line, the downtrend is considered to be intact.

A strong momentum in a trending market is usually accompanied by a steep trend line, with price continuously bouncing off the trend line.

Candlestick Size

In addition to using technical indicators, another way to identify strong momentum in a trending market is by observing the size of the candlesticks on a price chart.

If the trend is upwards and there is strong buying momentum, the candlesticks will be large and green, indicating that the price has moved significantly higher over a particular time period.

Conversely, if the trend is downwards and there is strong selling momentum, the candlesticks will be large and red, indicating that the price has moved significantly lower over a particular time period.

Large candlesticks are generally considered to be an indication of strong momentum, as they show that the price has moved significantly in a particular direction over a short period of time.

Momentum Indicators Remain in Overbought/Oversold Zones

In a strong trending market, momentum indicators can remain in the overbought/oversold zones for extended periods of time because the price of the asset is continuing to move in the same direction (either upwards or downwards) with little to no pullbacks or reversals.

For example, if the market is in an uptrend and there is strong buying momentum, the price of the asset may continue to rise without any significant retracements. This can cause momentum indicators, such as the RSI and Stochastic Oscillator, to remain in the overbought zone for a prolonged period.

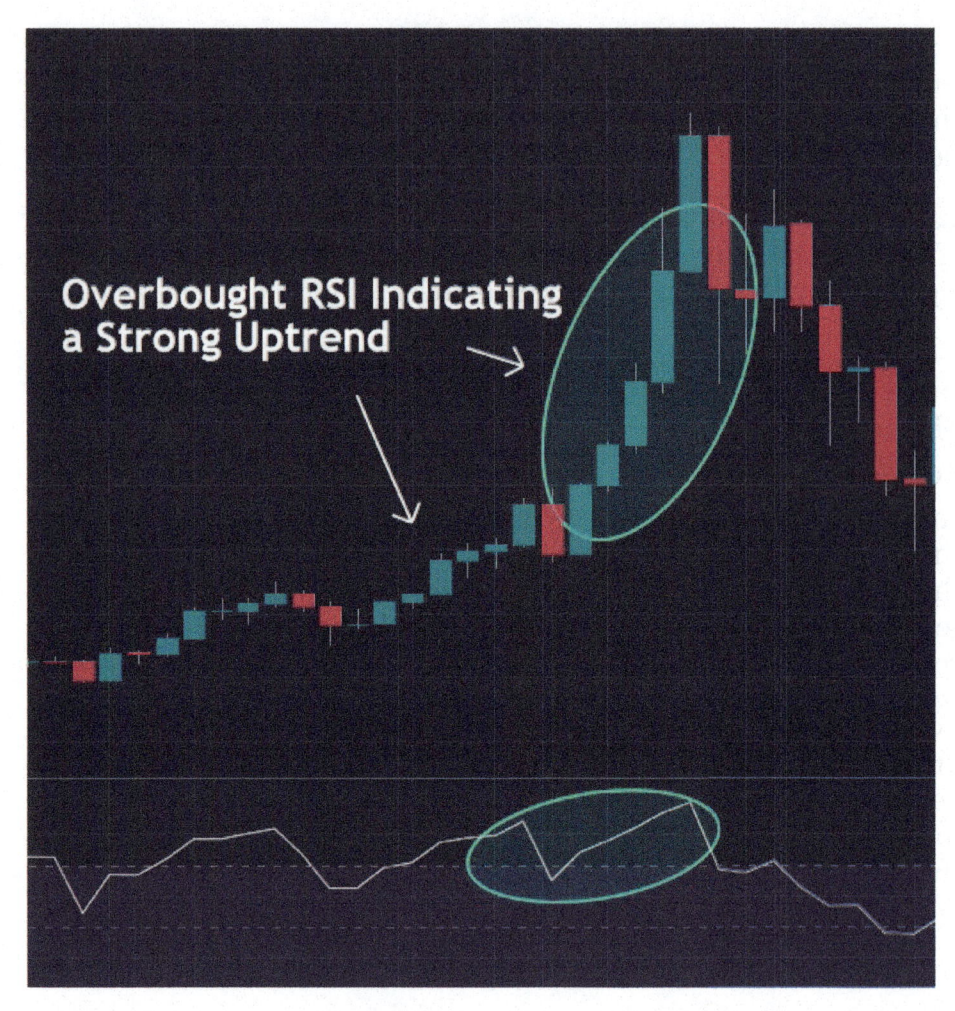

Example of the weekly RSI during the bitcoin 2017 bullmarket

Similarly, if the market is in a downtrend and there is strong selling momentum, the price of the asset may continue to fall without any significant retracements, causing momentum indicators to remain in the oversold zone.

This is why it's important to always wait for the momentum indicator to exit the overbought/oversold zone before using it as a valid signal.

Increasing Volume

Increasing volume can also be an indication of strong momentum in a trending market.

When the volume of an asset increases during an uptrend, it shows that there is strong buying pressure and that the trend is likely to continue.

Example of increasing buy volume, indicating increasing momentum

Similarly, when the volume increases during a downtrend, it shows that there is strong selling pressure and that the trend is likely to continue. A sudden spike in volume can also indicate a potential trend reversal, as it suggests that a large number of traders are entering or exiting the market at once.

It's important to note that increasing volume alone isn't enough to confirm a trend, but it can be used in combination with other technical indicators to confirm the strength of a trend.

The Role of Momentum in Market Reversals

A trend reversal is a change in the direction of a market trend. In other words, it is a change from an uptrend to a downtrend, or vice versa. Trend reversals can occur in any market and at any time, and they can have a significant impact on traders and investors.

Understanding the role of momentum in market reversals can help traders identify potential trend changes before they occur and make more informed trading decisions.

One of the key indicators of a trend reversal is a decrease in momentum. When momentum starts to decrease, it can indicate that the current trend is losing strength and a trend reversal may be imminent.

To predict trend reversals, traders can look out for several warning signs and reversal patterns, including:

1. Decreasing volume - A decrease in trading volume can indicate that traders are exiting their positions, signaling that the trend is losing strength.

2. Divergence - When the price of an asset and a momentum indicator are moving in opposite directions, it can be a sign that the trend is losing momentum.

3. Price closing below short-term moving averages - A move below the short-term moving average can indicate that the trend is losing momentum and a reversal may be imminent.

4. Break of key levels - If the price breaks through a key support or resistance level it can indicate that the trend has reversed.

5. Reversal patterns - Candlestick patterns such as the "hanging man" or "shooting star" can indicate a potential reversal in the trend.

Momentum plays a crucial role in identifying market reversals and traders should be aware of the warning signs.

Chapter 3: Identifying Winning Momentum Setups

In this chapter, we will discuss the importance of analyzing the market and identifying opportunities for profitable trades. We will examine different techniques for identifying breakouts, including the use of momentum indicators, price action analysis, and volume analysis.

We will also explore the importance of assessing risk and reward in momentum-based trades. This includes understanding the market conditions, such as support and resistance levels, and using stop-loss and take-profit orders to manage risk.

Additionally, we will look at different strategies that traders can use to identify winning momentum setups and maximize returns. Whether you're a novice trader or an experienced professional, this chapter will provide valuable insights into how to use momentum to identify profitable setups and improve your trading performance.

By the end of this chapter, you will have a better understanding of how to use momentum to identify profitable trades and increase your chances of success in the market.

Analyzing the Market and Identifying Opportunities

One of the key aspects of momentum trading is identifying opportunities in the market. This can involve analyzing various market indicators and price action to determine potential areas of momentum. In this chapter, we will discuss some of the ways traders can analyze the market and identify opportunities for momentum trading.

The first step in analyzing the market is to identify the overall trend. This can be done by using trend indicators, such as moving averages, to determine the direction of the market. Traders can also look for patterns in the price action, such as higher highs and lows, to confirm the direction of the trend. Once the trend has been identified, traders can then look for potential areas of momentum within that trend.

One of the most commonly used indicators for identifying momentum is the Relative Strength Index (RSI). The RSI compares the magnitude of recent gains to recent losses, and can be used to identify overbought or oversold conditions in the market. Other momentum indicators include the Moving Average Convergence Divergence (MACD) and the Stochastic Oscillator. These indicators can provide traders with valuable information about the momentum of the market, and can be used to identify potential trade setups.

Another way to identify opportunities in the market is through the use of chart patterns. Traders can look for patterns such as head and shoulders, triangles, and flags, which can indicate potential areas of momentum. These patterns can also be used to identify potential breakouts, which can signal the start of a new trend.

Once potential opportunities have been identified, traders should then assess the risk and reward of the trade. This can be done by using stop-loss orders and taking into account the volatility of the market. Traders should also consider the overall market conditions and any potential news or events that could affect the trade.

Trading Breakouts

One of the most effective ways to identify opportunities in the market is through the use of momentum to identify breakouts. A breakout is a move in the price of an asset that goes beyond a previous high or low, and can signal the start of a new trend. Breakouts can occur in both bullish and bearish markets and can be used by traders to enter or exit trades.

One of the key ways to use momentum to identify breakouts is by analyzing price action. Traders can look for patterns such as triangles, flags, and wedges, which can indicate a potential breakout. These patterns can also be used to identify potential support and resistance levels, which can be used to set stop-loss and take-profit levels.

Another important aspect of using momentum to identify breakouts is by using technical indicators.

Using Volume to Confirm Breakouts

Volume is a key metric that traders can use to identify breakouts. Volume is the number of shares or contracts traded in a certain period of time, and can be used to confirm the validity of a breakout. When a stock or asset experiences a breakout, it is usually accompanied by a significant increase in trading volume. This increased volume can serve as a confirmation that the breakout is legitimate and not just a temporary fluctuation in price.

There are several ways to use volume to identify breakouts. One way is to look for volume spikes, which are sudden increases in trading volume. These spikes can indicate that a large number of traders are buying or selling the stock, which can signal a potential breakout. Traders can also use volume indicators such as the On-Balance Volume (OBV) which is an indicator that uses volume to measure buying and selling pressure and this can help traders to identify if a breakout is likely.

Another way to use volume to identify breakouts is by looking for volume divergence. This occurs when the price of a stock is moving in one direction, but the volume is moving in the opposite direction. For example, if the price is moving higher, but the volume is decreasing, it could indicate that the rally is losing momentum and a potential breakout to the downside.

Traders can also look for volume-price trend (VPT) which is an indicator that uses volume to measure the buying and selling pressure and it can confirm if the breakout is strong or not. This can be done by plotting the volume on the y-axis, and the price on the x-axis. Traders can then analyze the slope of the line, and look for any changes in slope that could indicate a potential breakout.

Volume is a key metric that traders can use to identify breakouts. By looking for volume spikes, volume divergence, or volume-price trend, traders can increase their chances of success in identifying legitimate breakouts and potential opportunities in the market.

It is important to note that volume analysis should be used in combination with other technical analysis tools and indicators in order to increase the chances of successfully identifying a breakout.

Using the RSI to Confirm Breakouts

The Relative Strength Index (RSI) is a technical indicator that compares the magnitude of recent gains to recent losses to determine overbought or oversold conditions in the market. It can also be used to confirm and predict breakouts in the price of an asset.

When using the RSI to predict breakouts, traders can look for a resistance level on the RSI that breaks before a resistance level in price. This means that the RSI will break through a specific level, indicating that the underlying asset is gaining momentum, before the price breaks through a resistance level. This can be a powerful indicator of a potential breakout and can be used by traders to enter or exit trades.

For example, in a bullish market, if the RSI is consistently failing to reach the 70 level, it can indicate that there is resistance at that level. However, if the RSI breaks above 70 before the price breaks through a resistance level, it can indicate a potential breakout to the upside is imminent. Similarly, in a bearish market, if the RSI is consistently failing to reach the 30 level, it can indicate that there is resistance at that level. But if the RSI breaks below 30 before the price breaks through a resistance level, it can indicate a potential breakout to the downside is imminent.

Assessing risk and reward

One of the most important aspects of trading is assessing the risk and reward of a potential trade. This involves evaluating the potential loss and potential gain of a trade and determining if the trade is worth taking. Here we will discuss the concept of risk/reward ratio and how it can be used to determine the best time to enter a trade.

The risk/reward ratio is a ratio that compares the potential loss of a trade to the potential gain. It is typically expressed as a ratio, such as 1:2, which means that for every dollar at risk, the potential gain is two dollars. A higher risk/reward ratio indicates a higher potential reward for the same amount of risk.

When assessing the risk/reward ratio of a trade, traders should consider the potential profit and loss in relation to their overall trading strategy and risk management plan. This can involve setting stop-loss and take-profit levels, as well as considering the overall market conditions and any potential news or events that could affect the trade.

To enter a trade when there is a high likelihood of the trade working, traders should consider the following:

- Use multiple indicators and signals: Traders should use a combination of technical indicators, chart patterns, and price action signals to identify potential trade opportunities. This can help to confirm the signals generated by any one indicator and increase the likelihood of the trade working.

- Identify key levels of support and resistance: Traders should use support and resistance levels to identify potential entry and exit points for trades. This can help to increase the likelihood of the trade working by identifying areas where the price is likely to reverse or continue moving in the same direction.

- Wait for confirmations: Traders should wait for confirmations before entering a trade. This can include waiting for the price to break through a key level of resistance or for an indicator to generate a buy or sell signal.

- Assess the risk/reward ratio: Traders should always assess the risk/reward ratio of a trade before entering. This can help to ensure that the potential profit is greater than the potential loss.

Assessing the risk/reward ratio of a trade is an essential part of successful trading. By using multiple indicators and tools, identifying key levels of support and resistance, waiting for confirmations, and assessing the risk/reward ratio, traders can increase the likelihood of the trade working.

Steps for Identifying Good Entries and Exits Using Momentum Indicators

Identifying good entries and exits in a trading strategy using signals from momentum indicators can be done by following a few key steps:

1. Identify the direction of the trend: Use momentum indicators, such as the relative strength index (RSI) or stochastic oscillator, to identify the direction of the trend. A bullish trend is when prices are trending upward and a bearish trend is when prices are trending downward.

2. Look for overbought or oversold conditions: Use momentum indicators to identify when the market is overbought or oversold. Overbought conditions occur when prices have risen too quickly and are likely to fall, while oversold

conditions occur when prices have fallen too quickly and are likely to rise.

3. Identify entry signals: When the market is oversold and the trend is bullish, it can be a good opportunity to buy. Conversely, when the market is overbought and the trend is bearish, it can be a good opportunity to sell.

4. Identify exit signals: Use momentum indicators to identify when it is time to exit a trade. For example, if the RSI or stochastic oscillator indicates that the market is becoming overbought or oversold again, it may be time to exit the trade. Additionally, if the trend is changing direction, it is also a good time to exit the trade.

5. Place stop-loss orders: To limit potential losses, it is important to place stop-loss orders that will automatically close the trade if the market moves against you.

By following these steps, traders can use signals from momentum indicators to identify good entries and exits in their trading strategy.

However, it's worth noting that, it's important to keep in mind that no indicator is 100% accurate and it's always recommended to use other tools and analysis methods to confirm the signals.

Combining Short Term Momentum with Long Term Momentum

Combining short-term momentum with long-term momentum can be a good strategy in trading because it allows you to take advantage of both short-term price movements and long-term trends.

It is always better to trade in the direction of the long term momentum because:

- It helps to ensure that the trade is in line with the overall trend of the market.
- It reduces the risk of false signals
- The market movements on the shorter timeframes will be stronger in the direction of the long term momentum

In the example below, using a 1 hour timeframe stochastic oscillator (SO) in conjunction with a daily timeframe SO, the longer-term trend is represented by the daily SO.

When both the 1 hour and daily SO are indicating bullish trends and signals, traders can be more confident in entering a long position. This is because the longer-term trend is supporting the short-term trend, and the market is more likely to continue moving upwards.

Below is an example of a simple trading strategy using the SO (stochastic oscillator) using this method.

In this example we will use:

- 1 hour timeframe SO (stochastic oscillator), for identifying buy/sell signals
- Daily timeframe SO, for identifying and trading in the direction of the long term momentum
- Buy/sell signals will only be valid if they are in the same direction as the daily SO

Buy/Long When:

- The 1 hour SO is oversold(below 20) and crosses up out of the oversold zone
- The Daily SO is bullish (fast line above the slow line) and below 80 (not overbought)

Sell/Short When:

- The 1 hour SO is overbought (above 80) and crosses down out of the overbought zone
- The Daily SO is bearish (fast line below the slow line) and above 20 (not oversold)

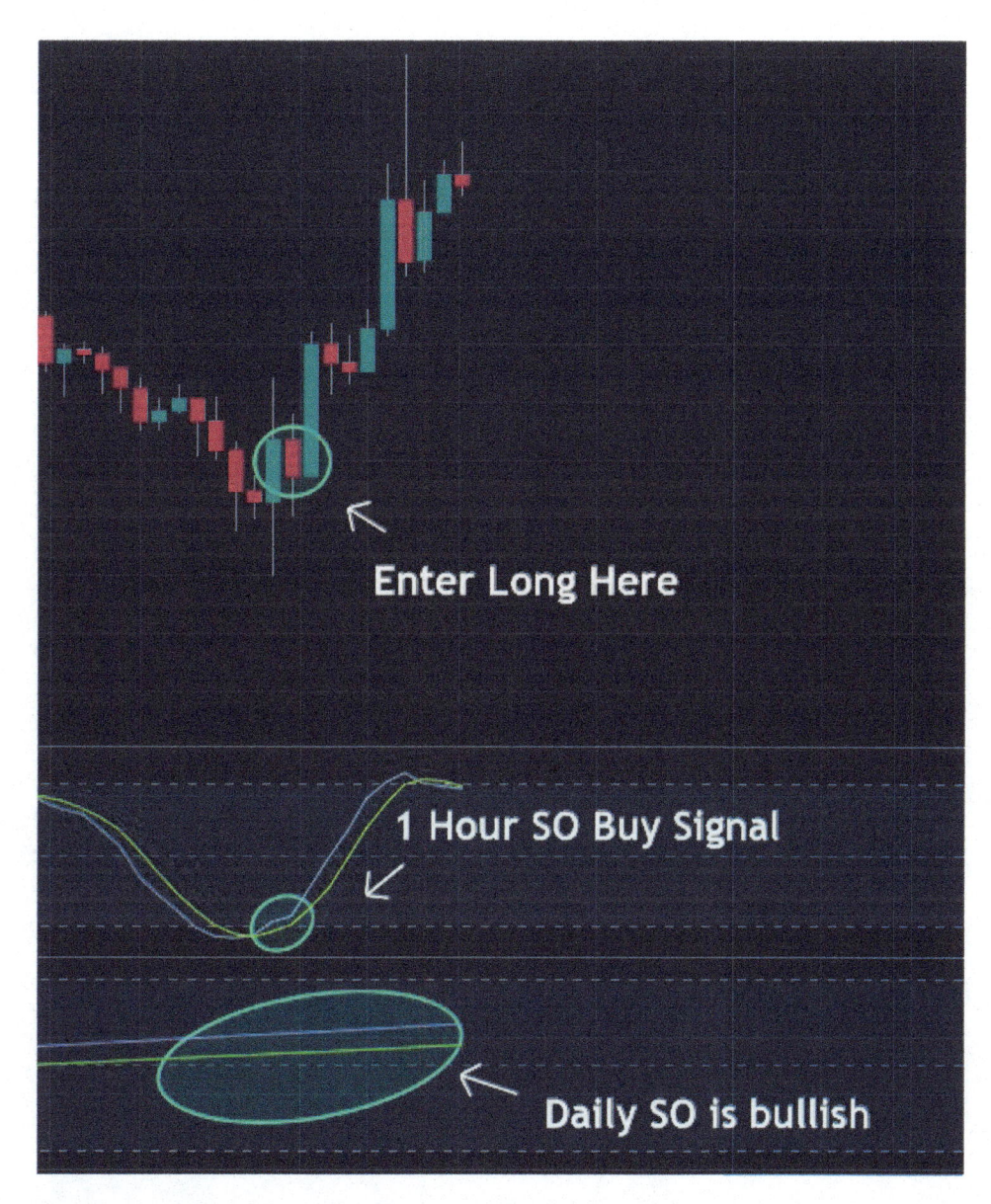

An example of a long trade using this strategy

Combining short-term momentum with long-term momentum can be a useful strategy in trading as it allows traders to take advantage of both short-term price movements and long-term trends.

By using a 1 hour timeframe stochastic oscillator (SO) in conjunction with a daily timeframe SO, traders can identify buy/sell signals that are in line with the overall trend of the market and reduce the risk of false signals.

Key Takeaways:

In this chapter we discussed the importance of identifying winning momentum setups in trading. By analyzing the market and identifying opportunities, traders can make informed decisions on when to enter and exit trades.

Breakouts and assessing risk and reward are also key factors to consider when using momentum indicators. Additionally, combining short term momentum with long term momentum can help to confirm a strong trading setup.

By following the steps outlined in this chapter, traders can increase their chances of success when using momentum indicators in their trading strategy.

Chapter 4: The Best TradingView Momentum Indicator Signals

How to Use These Signals

Momentum indicator signals are most effective when used in conjunction with other confirmation/trend following indicators, such as moving averages or volatility indicators (Bollinger bands, supertrend, etc).

For example, if a trader is using the overbought/oversold crossover signals from the stochastic oscillator, they may also use a moving average, to confirm the direction of the trend.

Here is how this might look:

- If price is above the 50 EMA, and the stochastic oscillator crosses up in the oversold zone, this is a valid buy signal

- If price is below the 50 EMA, and the stochastic oscillator crosses down in the overbought zone, this is a valid sell/short signal

Overall momentum indicators can provide very reliable and buy/sell signals, but they can produce whipsaw (false) signals, this is why it's important to use them in conjunction with other confirmation indicators and price action analysis.

How to Find These Indicator Signals

These are free indicators that other traders have created and coded on TradingView.

There are thousands of indicators on TradingView which other members have created, but these are the best momentum indicators I have found and use in my trading strategies.

To find these indicators on TradingView:

1. Make a TradingView account (TradingView.com), you can sign up for a free account if you don't want to pay.

2. Open up a chart on TradingView, and click on the "indicators" icon found at the top toolbar.

3. Then simply type in the indicator you are looking for in the search box.

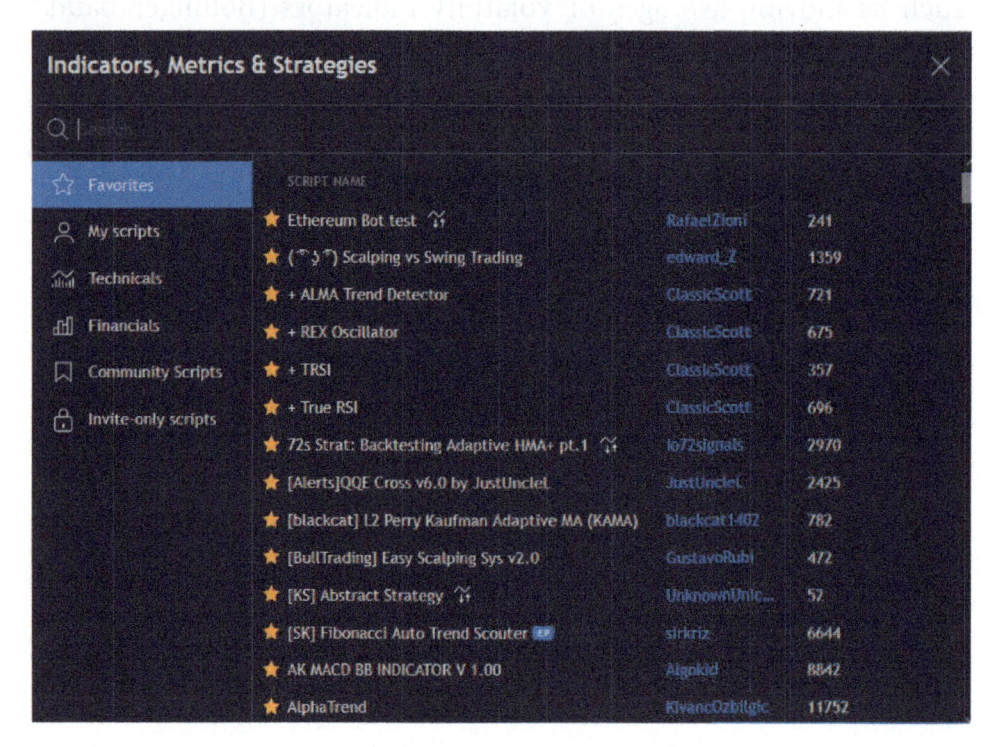

The TradingView indicator search box

Now that you know how to find these indicators, let's get started!

Momentum Indicator Buy/Sell Signal #1: TRIX With Moving Average

By: hgrams

To find this indicator type "TRIX With Moving Average - Didi's Needles setup" in the indicator search box

Overview:

The TRIX (Triple Exponential Average) indicator is similar to the Moving Average Convergence Divergence (MACD) indicator, but instead of using exponential moving averages, it uses a triple exponential moving average (TMA) to smooth out the price data.

The TRIX is calculated by taking the difference between the current EMA and the previous EMA, and then dividing the result by the previous EMA. The result is then plotted on a chart, with a positive TRIX indicating an upward trend and a negative TRIX indicating a downward trend.

The TRIX can be used in conjunction with other indicators, such as support and resistance levels, to confirm or refute trends. It also has a signal line which is a 9 period moving average of the TRIX, buy/sell signals occur when the TRIX crosses above or below the signal line.

Buy Signal:
- The signal (fast) line crosses above the TRIX (slow) line

Sell Signal:
- The signal (fast) line crosses below the TRIX (slow) line

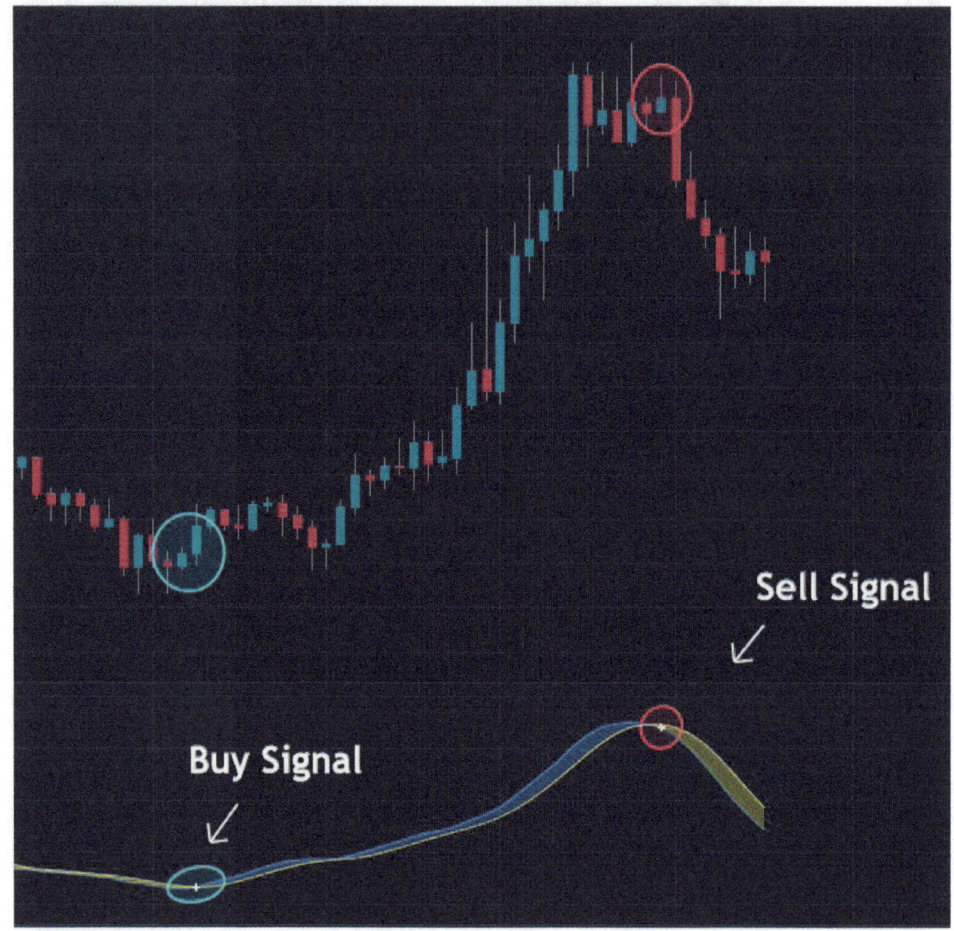

Example of buy (green circle) and sell (red circle) signals using the TRIX indicator

Momentum Indicator Buy/Sell Signal #2: Wavetrend in Dynamic Zones with Kumo Implied Volatility

By: AdonisWerther

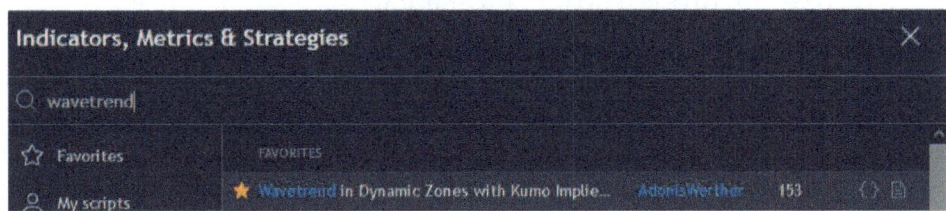

To find this indicator type "Wavetrend in Dynamic Zones with Kumo Implied Volatility" in the indicator search box

Overview:

The Wavetrend indicator is a technical analysis tool used in stock and forex trading to identify trends and potential trend changes. It is based on the idea that prices move in waves, and that these waves can be used to predict future price movements.

The Wavetrend indicator is a combination of several different indicators, including moving averages, relative strength index (RSI), and the Bollinger Bands. It is designed to provide traders with a clear, easy-to-read view of the current trend and potential trend changes.

This version of the Wavetrend indicator includes the dynamic OS/OB zones, and also indicates if volatility is increasing or decreasing.

Indicator Tip:

- Change the **channel length to 14**, and the **average length to 14** in the settings, this will reduce the amount of false signals.

Buy Signal:
- The Wavetrend indicator is in the buy zone (aqua colored zone)
- A green dot appears, this indicates bullish divergence and a cross up, this is a strong buy signal
- The white and blue dots are weaker signals (not as reliable)

Sell Signal:
- The Wavetrend indicator is in the sell zone (orange colored zone)
- A red dot appears, this indicates bearish divergence and a cross down, this is a strong sell signal

Example of buy (green circle) and sell (red circle) signals using this indicator

Momentum Indicator Buy/Sell Signal #3: L2 KDJ with Whale Pump Detector

By: blackcat1402

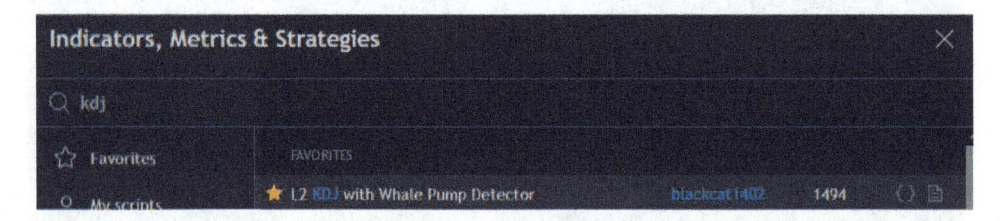

To find this indicator, type "L2 KDJ with Whale Pump Detector" in the indicator search box on TradingView (by blackcat1402)

Overview:

This indicator is a variation of the KDJ indicators, which a momentum oscillator similar to the stochastic oscillator. It uses the K and D lines from the stochastic, but also uses another line called the J line – hence the name KDJ.

Signals are generated when all three lines cross over in a certain diretction. The KDJ also includes overbought (above 100) and oversold (below 0) zones that can be used for entry/exit signals.

The signals from the KDJ will be the most reliable is sideways market conditions.

Indicator Tip:

- In the settings, remove the background colors on the KDJ

Buy Signal:
One of the following can be used-

- A green "B" label appears on the KDJ
- The three lines of the KDJ cross up

Sell Signal
One of the following can be used-

- A red "S" label appears on the KDJ
- All three lines cross down
- The KDJ crosses above 100 (overbought)

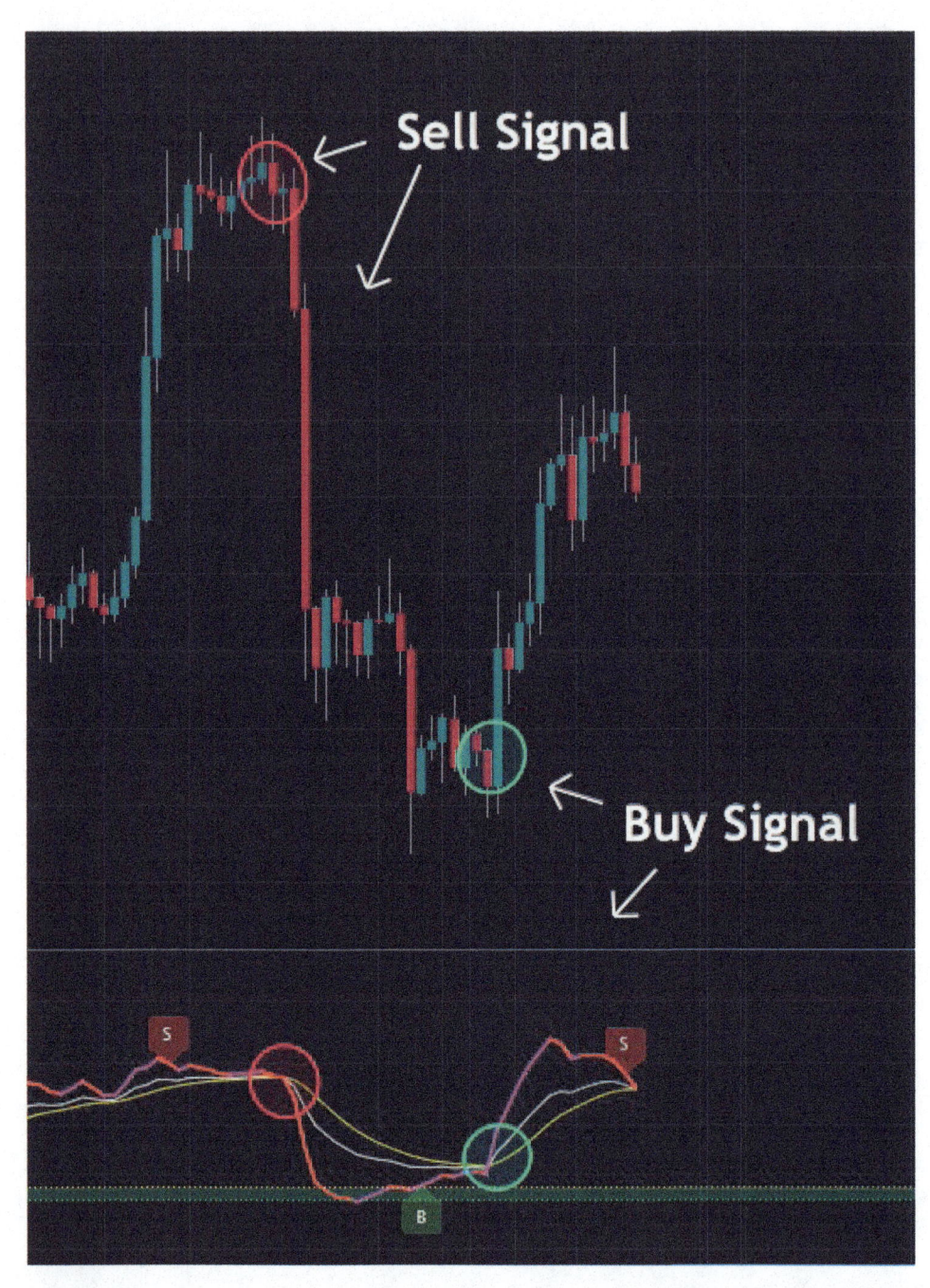

Example of buy/sell signals using L2 KDJ with Whale Pump Detector

Momentum Indicator Buy/Sell Signal #4: Bjorgum TSI

By: Bjorgum

To find this indicator type "Bjorgum TSI" in the indicator search box

Overview:

is similar to other momentum indicators such as the Relative Strength Index (RSI) or the Stochastic Oscillator, but it is considered to be a more advanced and accurate version of these indicators.

The TSI indicator is calculated by taking the difference between a fast and slow moving average of the asset's price, and then double smoothing the result. The double smoothing process helps to eliminate false signals and provide a more accurate representation of the asset's momentum.

Like other momentum indicators, TSI is a leading indicator, as it predicts future price movements based on the current momentum. This means that it can provide signals of potential price changes before they occur, making it a valuable tool for traders looking to enter or exit positions at the right time.

On the TSI indicator, signals occur when the fast line crosses above or below the slow, the slow line will change between red and blue colors to make it easier to identify these signals.

Buy Signal:
- The fast TSI line crosses above the slow line
- The Slow TSI line changes to blue

Sell Signal:
- The fast TSI line crosses below the slow line
- The Slow TSI line changes to red

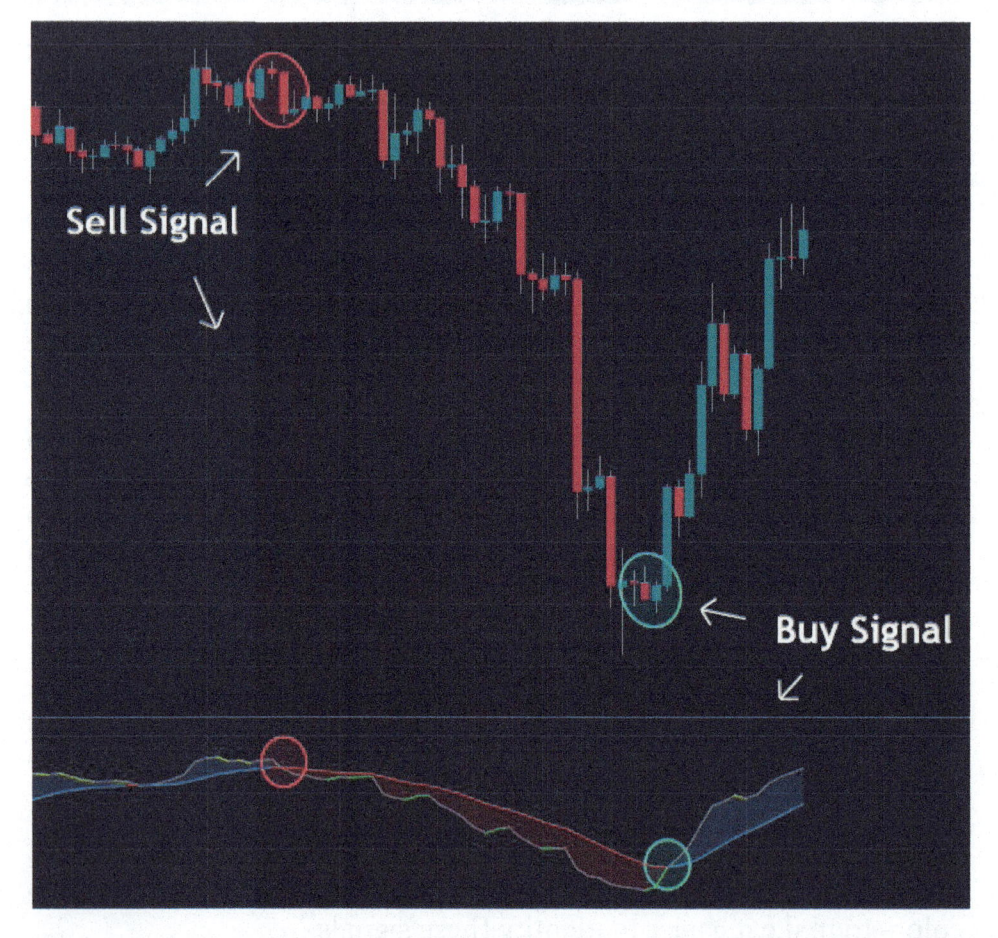

Example of buy (green circle) and sell (red circle) signals on the Bjorgum TSI indicator

Momentum Indicator Buy/Sell Signal #5: [N]RSIOMA

By: neutrid

To find indicator, type "[N]RSIOMA" in the indicator search box on TradingView (by neutrid)

Overview:

This is a smoother version of the RSI, and also includes a moving average to generate signals when the RSI crosses above or below the MA. The RSI color will also change between green and red colors depending on trend direction.

This indicator can also be used for identifying overbought/oversold signals.

Buy Signal:
Use one of the following-

- RSI crosses above the moving average
- The RSI is below 20 (oversold)
- The RSI color changes green

Sell Signal:
Use one of the following-

- The RSI crosses below the moving average
- The RSI is above 80 (overbought)
- The RSI color changes red

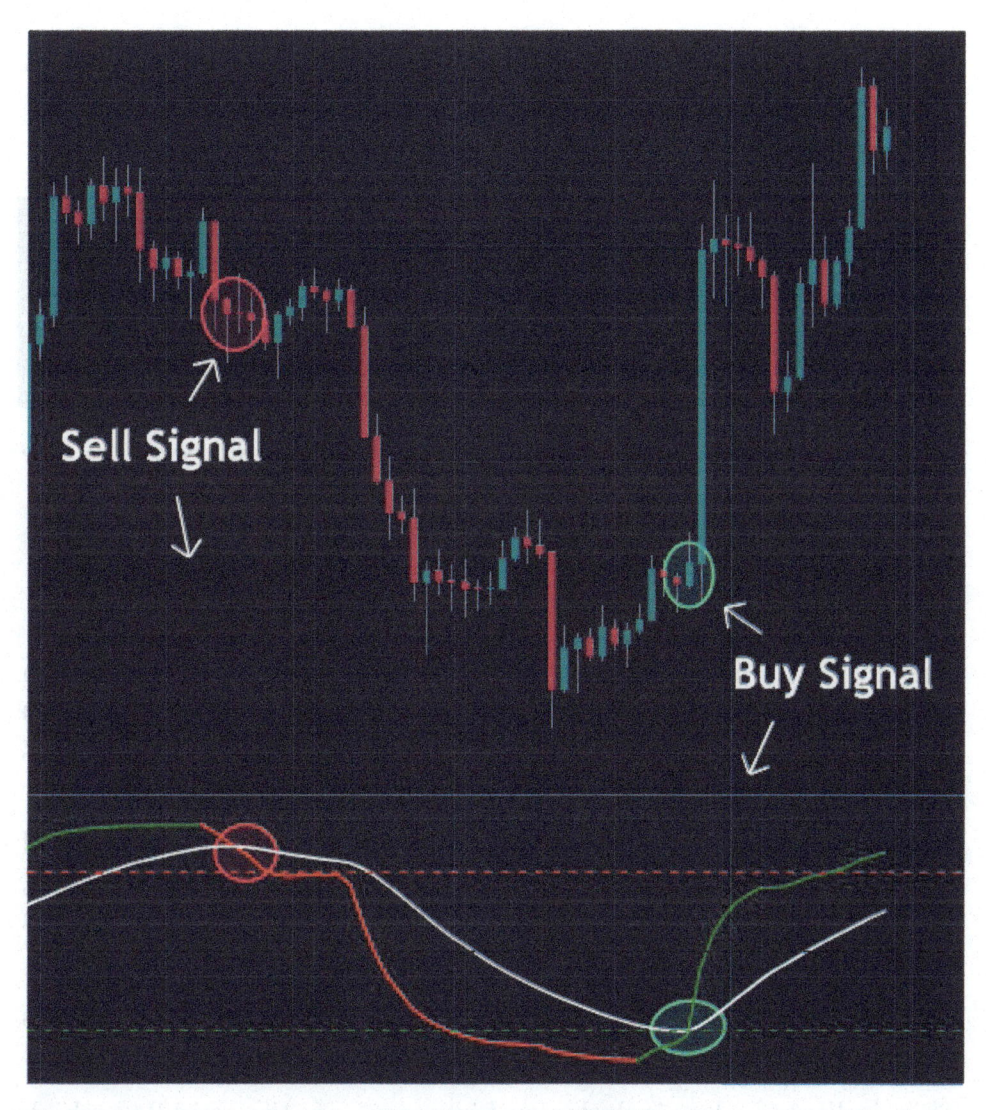

Example of buy/sell signals using [N]RSIOMA indicator

Momentum Indicator Buy/Sell Signal #6: TMO with TTM Squeeze

By: sskcharts

To find this indicator type "TMO with TTM Squeeze" in the indicator search box

Overview:

The TMO compares the current price of a security to its price a certain number of periods ago, and calculates the difference as a percentage. The resulting value is then smoothed using a moving average to reduce volatility and improve signal clarity.

The TMO will change between red and green colors when a signal occurs, and can be used to identify overbought/oversold conditions, as well as potential trend changes when the oscillator crosses down or up.

A good thing about this indicator is it produces fewer false signals then other momentum indicators like the MACD and RSI.

This indicator also includes a histogram in the middle, which represents the TTM indicator. This measures the volatility using the Keltner channels and the Bollinger bands. The histogram can be used to confirm the signals of the TMO.

Indicator Tip: For fewer false signals, change the TMO smooth length to 6

Buy Signal:
Use one of the following-

- The TMO crosses up out the oversold zone (-70)
- The TMO crosses up and turns green

Sell Signal:
Use one of the following-

- The TMO crosses down out the overbought zone (70)
- The TMO crosses down and turns red

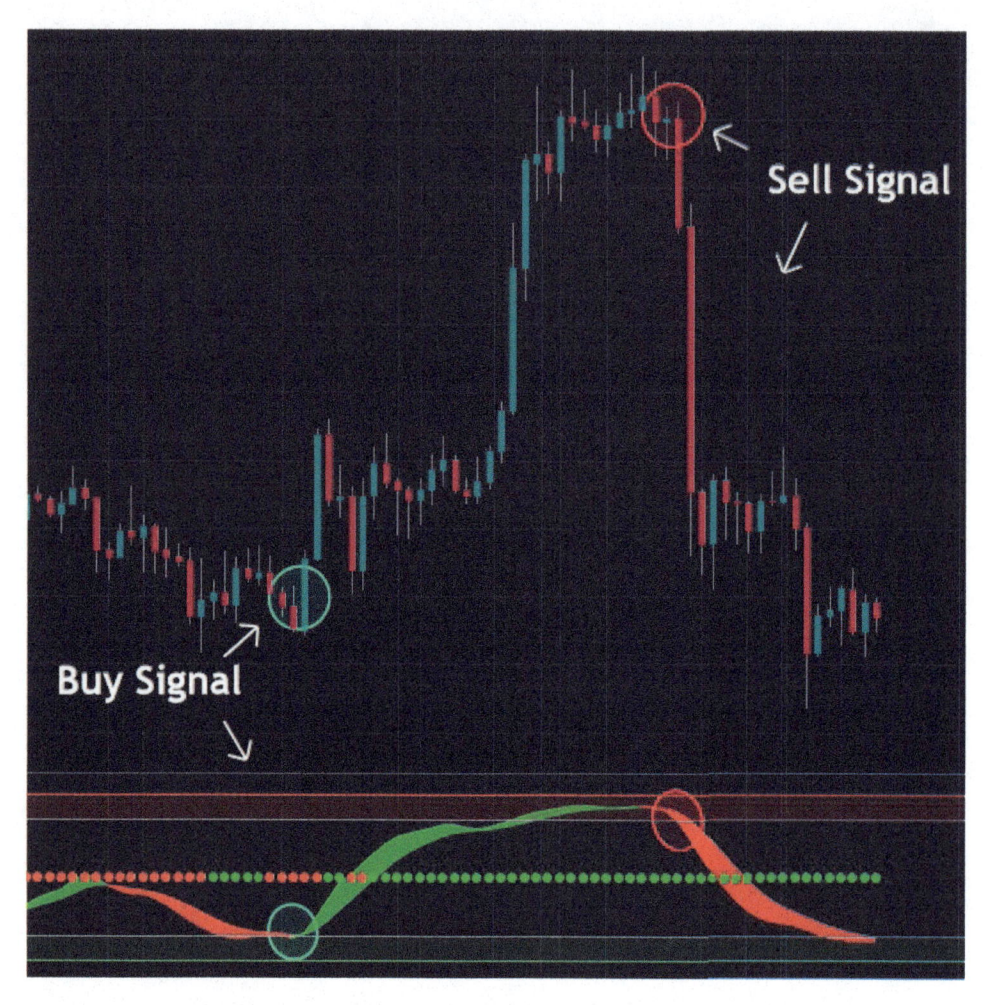

Example of buy (green circle) and sell (red circle) signals using the TMO with TTM Squeeze indicator

47

Momentum Indicator Buy/Sell Signal #7: Filtered RSI Divergence Finder

By: scarf

To find indicator, type "Filtered RSI Divergence Finder" in the indicator search box on TradingView (by scarf)

Overview:

This indicator is based on using RSI divergence to predict tops and bottoms. When RSI divergence is identified a signal will appear on the chart.

When this indicator detects divergence, a green buy signal will appear under a candle for bullish divergence and a red sell signal will appear above a candle for bearish divergence.

Long/Buy Signal:
- Green "R" label appears under a candle

Short/Sell Signal:
- Red "R" label appears above a candle

Long and short entries using the Filtered RSI Divergence Finder indicator

Momentum Indicator Buy/Sell Signal #8: Williams %R

By: stuehmer

To find this indicator, type "Williams %R" in the indicator search box on TradingView (by stuehmer)

Overview:

The Williams %R indicator, is a technical indicator that is used to measure overbought and oversold levels in the market. The indicator ranges from -100 to 0, with -100 being the most oversold and 0 being the most overbought.

When the Williams %R is overbought, it indicates that the market is likely to experience a trend reversal and prices may start to fall. On the other hand, when the Williams %R is oversold, it indicates that the market is likely to experience a trend reversal and prices may start to rise.

This version of the Williams %R also includes a moving average to generate buy/sell signals when the Williams %R crosses above or below it.

Overbought/oversold signals or moving average crossover signals can be used on this indicator.

Long Entry:

The Williams %R crosses above the EMA

The Williams %R crosses up out of the oversold zone (-80)

Long Exit:

The Williams%R crosses above -20 (overbought)

The Williams %R crosses below the EMA

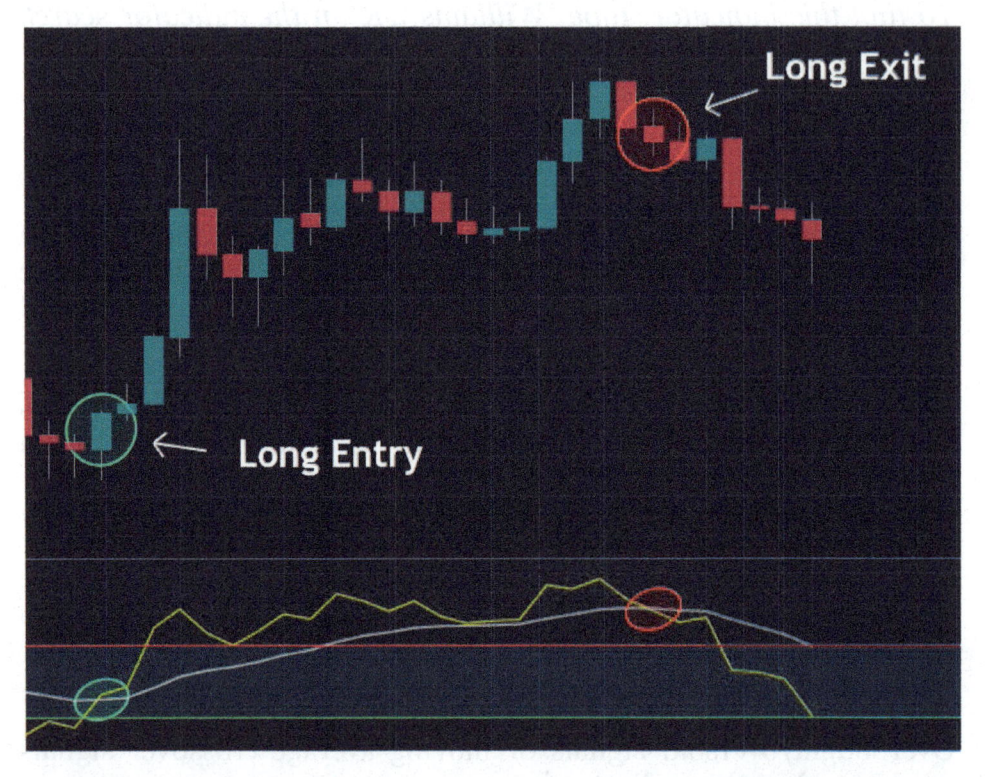

Example of buy (green circle) and sell (red circle) signals using the Williams %R indicator

Momentum Indicator Buy/Sell Signal #9: Quantitative Qualitative Estimation QQE

By: KivancOzbilgic

To find this indicator, type "Quantitative Qualitative Estimation QQE" in the indicator search box on TradingView

Overview:

The QQE indicator is made up of two lines: the first line is the smoothed relative strength index (RSI), which is calculated using a smoothed moving average, and the second line is a signal line, which is calculated using a moving average of the first line.

When the smoothed RSI line is above the signal line, it indicates a bullish trend and generates a buy signal. Conversely, when the smoothed RSI line is below the signal line, it indicates a bearish trend and generates a sell signal.

This indicator will display "buy" and "sell" labels on the indicator when a signal occurs making it easy to use and identify signals.

Buy Signal:
- The fast QQE line crosses above the slow line (green "Buy" arrow appears)

Sell Signal:
- The fast QQE line crosses below the slow line (red "sell" arrow appears)

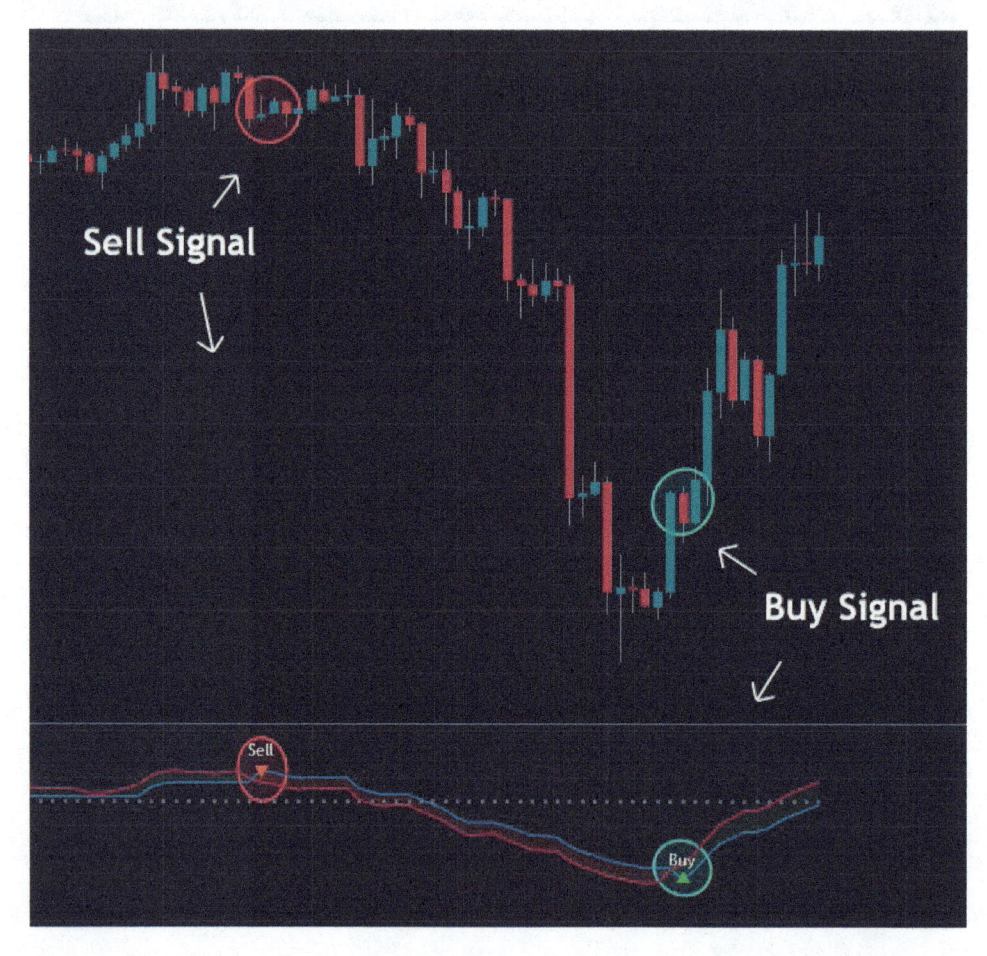

Example of buy and sell signals occurring on the QQE indicator

Chapter 5: Momentum Trading Strategies

In this chapter, we will cover some highly profitable momentum trading strategies. These strategies use momentum indicators for entries/exits along with at least one confirmation indicator to confirm the entry signal.

Before using these strategies it is highly recommended that you backtest and paper trade these strategies first. This is important because it allows you to verify that the strategy works, and will help you familiarize yourself with the strategy.

A good momentum day trading strategy typically includes the following components:

1. A momentum indicator: This is a technical indicator that helps to identify the strength and direction of a stock's price movement. Common momentum indicators include the Relative Strength Index (RSI), Moving Average Convergence Divergence (MACD), and the Stochastic Oscillator.

2. A trend-following indicator: This is an indicator that helps to identify the direction of the overall market trend. Common trend-following indicators include the Moving Average and the Ichimoku Cloud.

3. A confirmation indicator: This is an indicator that helps to confirm the signals generated by the momentum, trend-following, and volatility indicators. The confirmation indicator can be another technical indicator or a chart pattern that confirms the signal generated by the primary indicators.

4. A risk management plan: A good momentum day trading strategy should include a plan for managing risk. This can include setting stop-loss orders, using position sizing to limit potential losses, and diversifying your portfolio.

5. Entry and exit rules: A good momentum day trading strategy should have specific rules for entering and exiting trades. These rules should be based on the signals generated by the momentum, trend-following, and volatility indicators, and should take into account the overall market conditions.

By incorporating these components into your trading strategy, you can develop a more effective approach to momentum day trading that is tailored to your individual needs and goals. Additionally, using a confirmation indicator can increase the probability of a successful trade by providing an additional layer of confirmation before entering a trade, this can help you avoid false signals.

However, it is important to keep in mind that no strategy is fail-proof, and it's important to continue to monitor and adjust your strategy as necessary to adapt to changing market conditions.

Momentum Strategy #1: TSI + DEMA

Strategy Overview:

This strategy uses signals from the TSI indicator for entries/exits, and the DEMA (double exponential moving average) as a secondary confirmation indicator to confirm the signals of the TSI.

A 500 period SMA is used to trade in the direction of the long term trend.

Strategy Indicators:

- Bjorgum TSI (by Bjorgum on TradingView) – Change the TSI speed to slow
- 40 period DEMA (double exponential moving average)
- 500 period SMA (simple moving average)

Buy/Long Conditions:

- Price is above the 500 SMA
- The TSI crosses up
- Enter when price closes above the DEMA

Exit/Take Profit When:

Choose one of the following-

- Price closes below the DEMA
- The TSI crosses down

Sell/Short Conditions:
- Price is below the 500 SMA
- The TSI crosses down
- Enter when price closes below the DEMA

Exit/Take Profit When:

Choose one of the following-

- Price closes above the DEMA
- The TSI crosses up

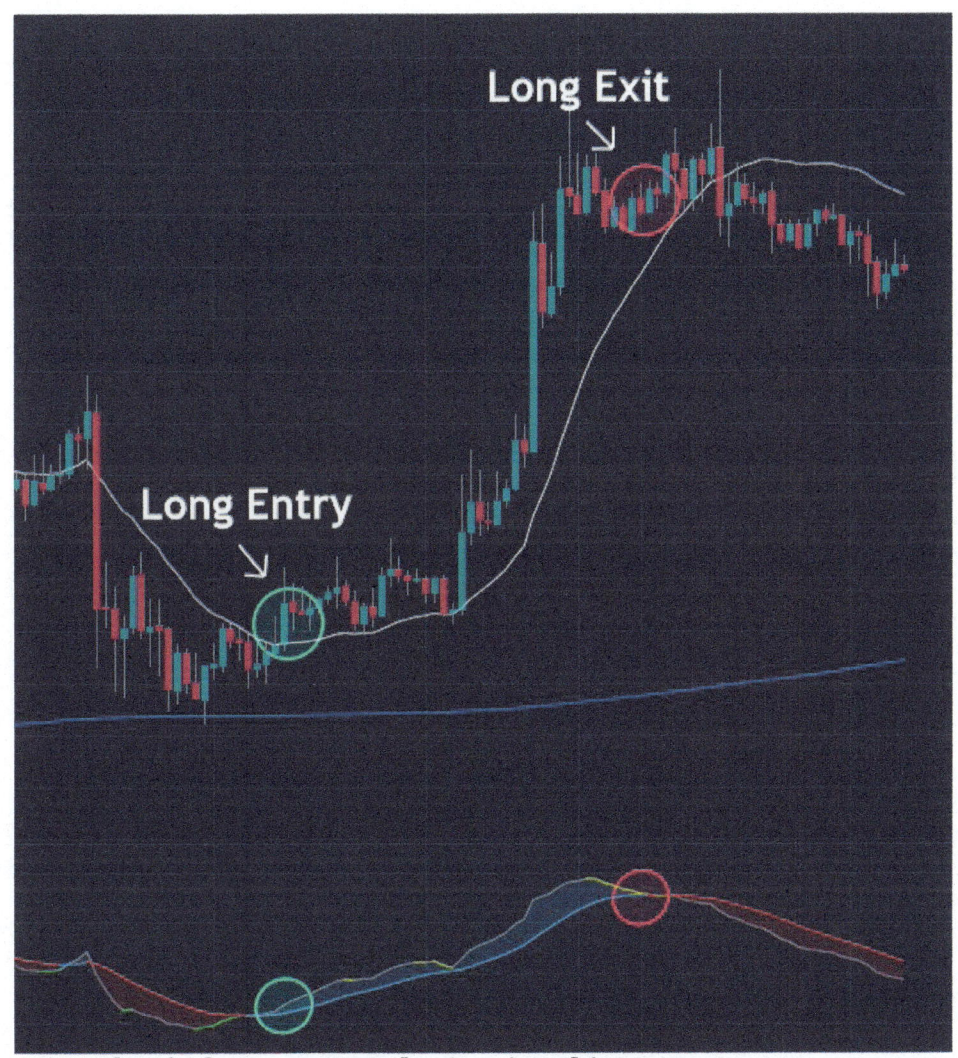

Example of a long entry and exit using this strategy

Momentum Strategy #2: Double MACD Strategy

Overview

This strategy uses two Moving Average Convergence Divergence (MACD) indicators; The first uses a 1 hour timeframe for entries and the other uses a daily timeframe for identifying and trading with the long term momentum.

A 20 period moving average is also used to confirm entries.

Required Indicators:
- MACD - 1 hour timeframe
- MACD - Daily timeframe
- 20 period SMA

Buy/Long Conditions:
- The daily MACD is bullish (fast line above the slow line)
- The 1 hour MACD crosses up
- Enter when price closes above the 30 SMA
- Place stop loss under the low of the entry candle

Exit/Take Profit When:

Choose one of the following-

- Price closes below the 30 SMA (recommended)

Or

- The 1 hour MACD crosses up

Sell/Short Conditions

- The daily MACD is bearish (fast line below the slow line)
- The 1 hour MACD crosses down
- Enter when price closes below the 30 SMA
- Place stop loss under the low of the entry candle

Exit/Take Profit When:

Choose one of the following-

- Price closes above the 30 SMA (recommended)

Or

- The 1 hour MACD crosses up

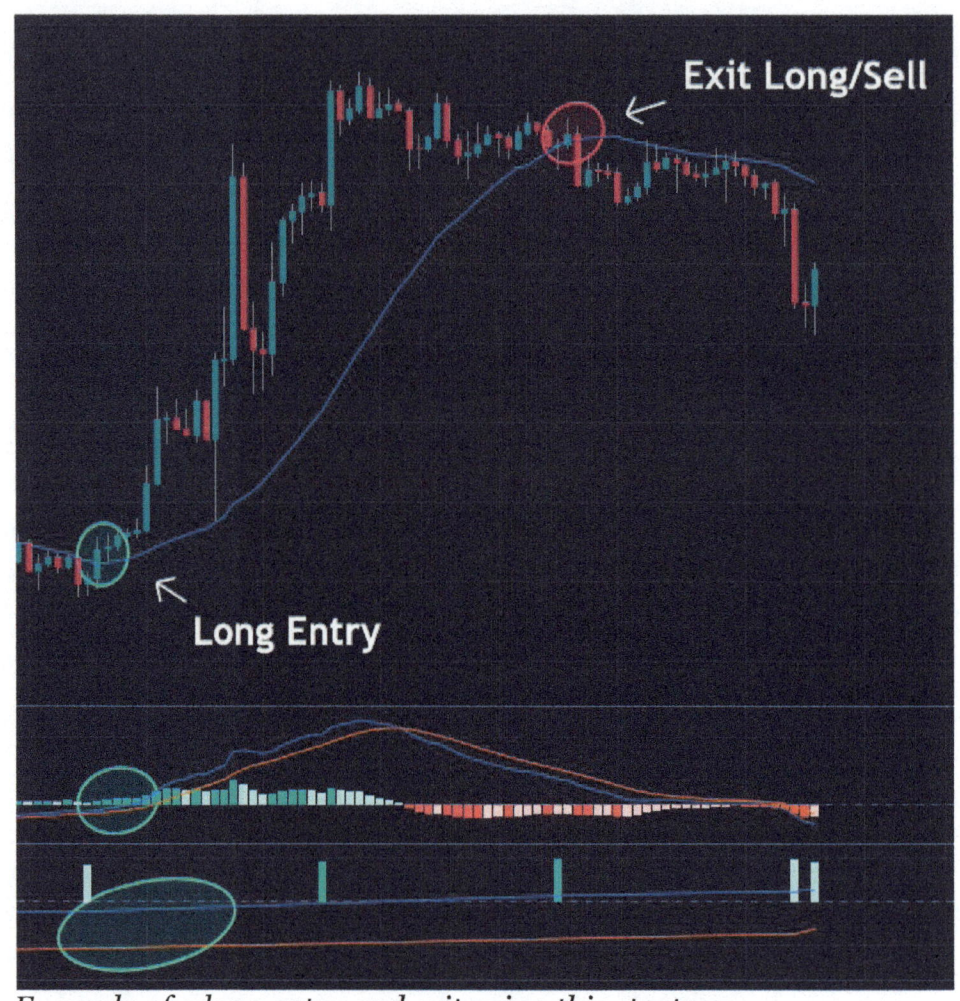

Example of a long entry and exit using this strategy

Momentum Strategy #3: UT Bot + KDJ

Strategy Overview:

This strategy uses the UT Bot Alert indicator for accurately identifying trends, and the KDJ indicator for perfect entries in the trend.

Once you enter the trend, you can decide to ride it out or scalp it for a quicker trade depending on your trading style and preference.

This strategy also uses a 200 SMA to trade in the direction of the overall trend.

Strategy Indicators:

- UT Bot Alerts (by QuantNomad on TradingView)

    *Change settings - Key Value = 3, ATR period = 30

- L2 KDJ with Whale Pump Detector (by blackcat 1402 on TradingView)

    *You can turn off the background colors on the KDJ in the settings

- 200 SMA

Buy/Long Conditions:
- Price is above the 200 SMA
- Candle color is green and a buy label appears below a candle
- Enter when a green "B" letter appears on the KDJ, or all three KDJ lines cross up.

Exit/Take Profit When:

Use one of the following-

- The KDJ crosses down
- The KDJ overbought (above 80)
- A sell signal from the UT bot occurs

Sell/Short Conditions:
- Price is below the 200 SMA
- Candle color is red and a sell label appears above a candle
- Enter when a red "S" letter appears on the KDJ, or all three KDJ lines cross down.

Exit/Take Profit When:

Use one of the following-

- The KDJ crosses up
- The KDJ oversold (below 20)
- A buy signal from the UT bot occurs

Example of a long entry and exit signal using this strategy

Momentum Strategy #4: TMO + Hull Strategy

Strategy Overview:

This trading strategy uses a 50 period Hull Moving Average (HMA) as the entry indicator, with the TMO indicator serving as a confirmation of the HMA signal.

The 200 Simple Moving Average (SMA) is used to identify the overall trend of the market, providing additional context for the HMA and TMO signals.

Strategy Indicators:
- 50 period HMA
- TMO with TTM Squeeze (by sskcharts on TradingView)
- 200 SMA

Buy/Long Conditions:
- Price is above the 200 SMA
- The TMO is oversold (below -70)
- Enter when price closes above the 50 HMA

Exit/Take Profit When:

Use one of the following-

- Price closes below the 50 HMA
- The TMO crosses down from the overbought zone

Sell/Short Conditions:
- Price is below the 200 SMA
- The TMO is overbought (above 70)
- Enter when price closes below the 50 HMA

Exit/Take Profit When:

Use one of the following-

- Price closes above the 50 HMA
- The TMO crosses up from the oversold zone

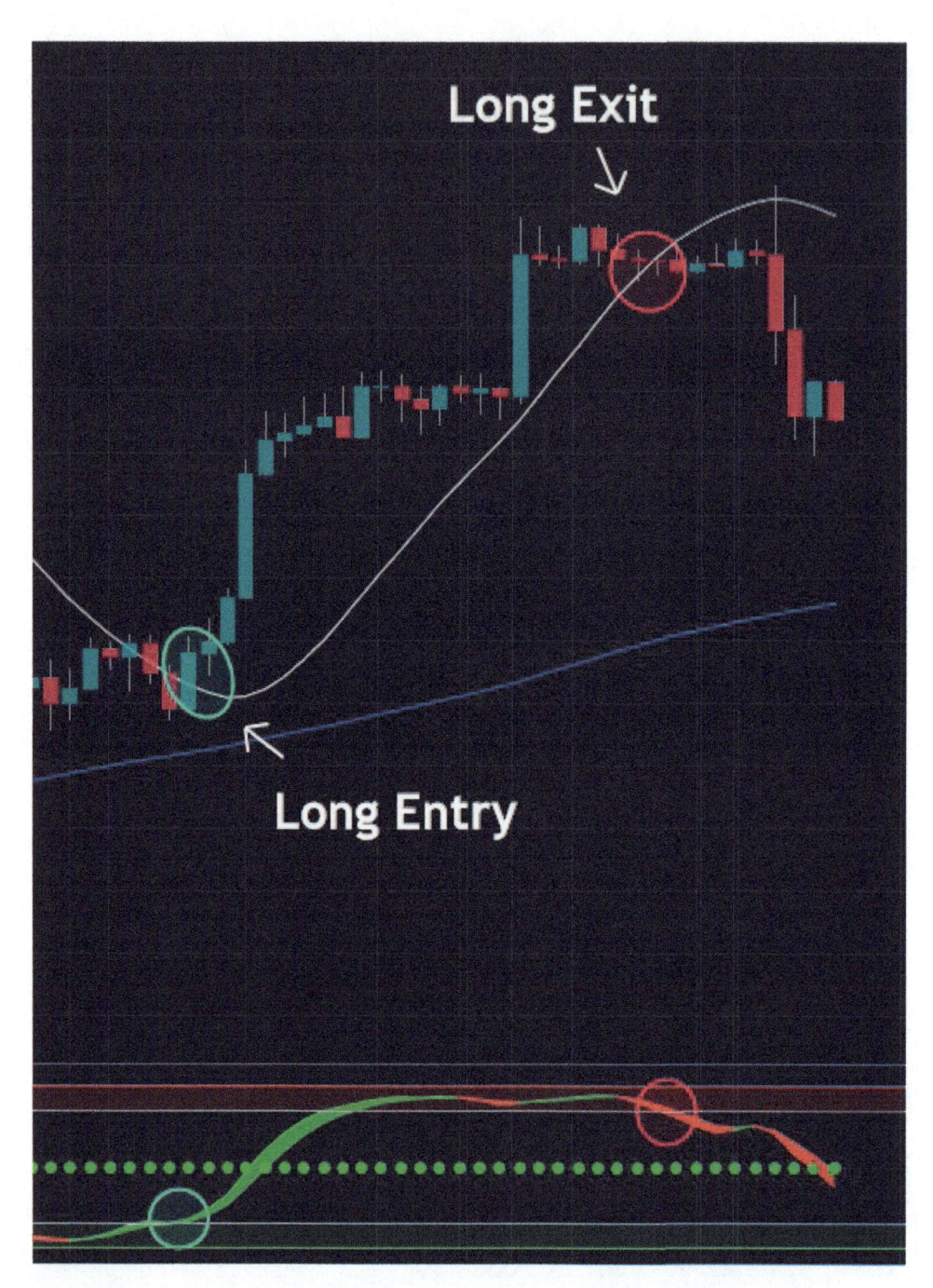

Example of a long entry/exit using this strategy

Momentum Strategy #5: Williams %R Scalping Strategy

Strategy Overview:

This is a scalping strategy using the CM pivot bands indicator and the Williams %R (the willy) indicators for scalping short term price swings in the market.

When price touches the top or bottom of the CM pivot bands it will likely act as support/resistance levels where price will reverse.

The Williams %R indicator used in this strategy is similar to the RSI. This version of the Williams %R indicator uses a moving average for identifying signals.

This strategy will work the best in sideways/rangebound markets, the ADX is used to filter out trending market conditions.

Strategy Indicators:

- CM Pivot Bands V1 (by ChrisMoody on TradingView)

    *Change the length to 20

- Williams %R (by Stuehmer on TradingView)
- ADX

Buy/Long Conditions:
- The ADX is below 25
- Candles are closing in the bottom green band
- Enter long when the Williams%R crosses above the MA

Exit/Take Profit When:

Use one of the following -

- The Williams %R crosses below the MA
- The Williams %R is overbought (above -80)
- Price is touching the top band

Sell/Short Conditions
- The ADX is below 25
- Candles are closing in the top red band
- Enter short when the Williams%R crosses below the MA

Exit/Take Profit When:

Use one of the following -

- The Williams %R crosses above the MA
- The Williams %R is oversold (below -40)
- Price is touching the bottom band

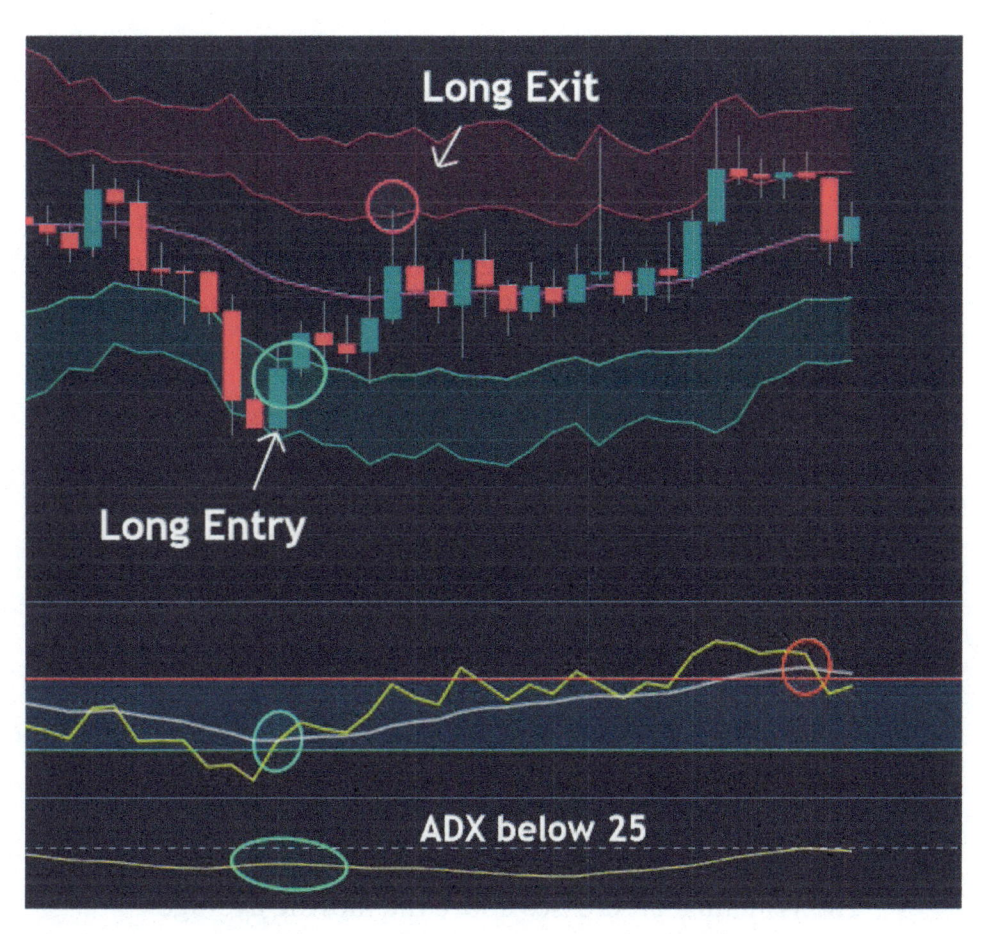

Example of a long entry and exit using this strategy

Momentum Strategy #6: HalfTrend + Williams %R

Overview:

This strategy uses the Williams%R indicator for buy/sell signals, with the Halftrend indicator being used to confirm the signals. The 500 EMA is used to identify and trade in the direction of the long term trend.

Strategy Indicators:
- 500 EMA
- HalfTrend (by everget)
- Williams %R – Smoothed (By: PtGambler)

Buy/Long Conditions:
- Price is above the 500 EMA
- The Williams %R crosses above the moving average
- Enter long when a buy signal (blue arrow) appears on the HalfTrend indicator

Exit/Take Profit When:

One of the following occurs-

- The Williams %R crosses below the moving average
- A sell signal (red arrow) appears on the HalfTrend indicator

Sell/Short Conditions:
- Price is below the 500 EMA
- The Williams %R crosses below the moving average
- Enter short when a sell signal (red arrow) appears on the HalfTrend indicator

Exit/Take Profit When:

One of the following occurs-

- The Williams %R crosses above the moving average
- A buy signal (blue arrow) appears on the HalfTrend indicator

A long entry and exit using this strategy

Momentum Strategy #7: BB + VWAP and Stochastic

Overview:
This strategy uses the stochastic oscillator for buy/sell signals, and the Bollinger bands to confirm these signals. The VWAP is used to trade with the longer term trend.

This strategy works best on the 5 minute timeframe.

Indicators Used in Strategy:
- VWAP (volume weighted average price)

    remove the bands on the VWAP, with only the VWAP line visible

- Bollinger Bands

    Change the settings to: StdDev = 1.5

- Stochastic Oscillator

    change settings to: %K Length = 7, %K Smoothing = 4, %D Smoothing = 3

Long Entry Conditions:
- Price is above the VWAP
- A candle closes below the bottom Bollinger band
- The Stochastics are below 20 (oversold)
- Enter when a candle closes above the bottom Bollinger band, place stop loss below the entry candle

Exit/Take Profit When:
- One of the following occurs-
- Price touches the top Bollinger band
- The Stochastic is in the overbought zone (above 80)

Sell/Short Entry Conditions:
- Price is below the VWAP
- A candle closes above the top Bollinger band
- The Stochastics are above 80 (overbought)
- Enter when a candle closes below the top Bollinger band, place stop loss above the entry candle

Exit/Take Profit When:

Choose one of the following:
- Price touches the bottom Bollinger band
- The Stochastic is in the oversold zone (below 20)

A long entry and exit using this strategy

Conclusion

In conclusion, momentum trading is a powerful technique that can help traders identify potential opportunities and make informed decisions in the market.

Through the use of momentum indicators and other tools, traders can analyze market trends and identify strong momentum setups that may indicate potential buying or selling opportunities.

By combining short-term and long-term momentum indicators, traders can gain a more comprehensive understanding of market conditions and make more informed trades. Additionally, by using the strategies and techniques outlined in this guide, traders can develop a more effective momentum trading strategy that is tailored to their individual needs and goals.

Overall, this guide has provided a comprehensive overview of the key concepts and techniques involved in momentum trading and has demonstrated how traders can use these tools to make profitable trades in the market.

Final Tips for Trading Momentum:

- Always be aware of market conditions and the broader economic context. Momentum indicators and strategies can be useful, but they should be used in conjunction with other forms of analysis and always in the context of the current market conditions.

- Use momentum indicators to identify potential buying or selling opportunities, but don't rely on them solely. Remember to also consider other technical indicators, chart patterns, and fundamental factors when making trading decisions.

- Be patient and disciplined in your approach. Momentum trading can be profitable, but it also requires patience and discipline to wait for the right opportunities and to stick to your trading plan.

- Always be aware of risk and have a plan for managing it. It's crucial to have a plan for managing risk and to always consider the potential loss before entering a trade.

- Finally, be adaptable and always willing to learn. Trading is constantly changing, and strategies that work well in one market may not work as well in another. Stay up to date with the latest market trends and research and adapt your trading strategies accordingly.

Made in the USA
Las Vegas, NV
02 October 2024